COPING WITH THE LOSS OF A PET

Coping
With The Loss
Of A Pet

A Gentle Guide For All Who Love A Pet

CHRISTINA M. LEMIEUX, Ph.D.

PHOTOGRAPHY BY DENIS G. LEMAY

Wallace R. Clark

This book is dedicated to
devoted pet lovers everywhere.

Printed in the United State of America.

FIRST EDITION

Library of Congress Cataloging in Publication Data

Lemieux, Christina M.
    COPING WITH THE LOSS OF A PET.

    1. Pets. 2. Consolation. 3. Grieving. 4. Bereavement.

I. Title.
88-92785
ISBN 0-9622158-0-5

Contents

Preface

The death of a beloved pet is a devastating emotional experience. If you have lost a pet, you know how true this is.

Sad to say, this experience is in store for all of us who have a pet we love and cherish. But we do not have to go through this experience alone.

This little book was written to keep you company and provide some suggestions to help you in your time of grief. This book will also give some gentle guidance to those of you who are comforting others in their grieving.

Although the discussions included here feature dogs and cats, the overall message is intended to apply to nearly all pets and to those special people everywhere who are devoted pet lovers.

I. Alone

My little old dog;
A heart-beat at my feet.

Edith Wharton

Alone.

Something important has gone out of your life. You have lost your pet. And something big has been added to your life: pain. There is the overall aching hollowness that pervades your waking moments and sometimes even your dreams. And the specific stabbing pain that often strikes you like a sharp knife when you walk into the house and no brown furry form hurtles across the room to give you a joyful welcome. When you are sitting on the living room couch reading or lost in thought, you unconsciously reach out to feel that soft and sensitive head beside you. But it is not there!

Each day you find that the time in your schedule you had always set aside especially for your pet is now ''empty time'' and it now hangs heavily upon you. No more are the needs of your pet a part of your daily considerations in shopping, in recreation, or in the time spent just being there.

What are you going to do? Should you try to tell other people what you are going through? Would that help in some way? You're not at all sure about this. What if they say, "I know exactly how you feel." How in the world can they? Unless they have lost a beloved pet themselves, how can they possibly know how you feel? And it won't help a bit if they say, "Well, what you need to do is go our right now and get a new kitten." To replace Susie? Nothing can ever replace Susie. The very thought makes the pain worse.

Some people might even laugh if you were to tell them what is really bothering you. You don't need to hear, "After all, it was only a dog," or, "Why are you making such a fuss over just a cat," or, "It's not as if you have lost your best friend." But the fact is, one of your best friends (maybe the best) *has* died, and others just do not understand.

My friend David had as a pet and companion a beautiful black Labrador retriever named Max. David's love for Max began the day Max, as a small puppy, came into

David's life. David later married and had children and Max's love and loyalty became an important part of their family experience.

When old age and failing health finally caused Max's death, everyone in David's family was saddened. But it soon became obvious that Max's death had a unique and unmatched effect on David. Their's was the really special relationship.

It may be that others are missing your pet, too. Your family, your friends, maybe they also loved Inky. But they had their relationship with him and you had yours. Like my friend David, you miss your pet in a very special way. And you feel very much alone in your distress.

II. A Time To Grieve

1. You Need To Grieve.

I could discern clearly, even at that early age,
the essential difference between people who are
kind to dogs and people who really love them.
                                        Frances P. Cobbe

Now you need to allow yourself, and even encourage yourself, to grieve. Let yourself feel the pain of loss, and express what you are feeling to yourself and to others.

To feel miserable at a time like this is both normal and natural. Don't pronounce a verdict on yourself. And don't think, ''Why am I feeling so awful? There must be something wrong with me.'' The reason you are feeling so bad is because you are missing and continuing to love the pet you lost.

It is now that many people tend to deny or otherwise attempt to avoid what their mind and heart tell them they are feeling. Such an approach to your grieving is not helpful, nor is it an honest reflection of what is taking place.

Do not be ashamed of being a caring person. All those experiences you shared together with your pet created a bond between you, a bond that became a continuing source of good feelings. Those walks you took together. The games you played together. The hard times in your life when he was always there, standing by you. The times she distracted you from your troubles, making you laugh at her antics. Above all, those times when you just kept each other silent company. These were all parts of the way you cared for one another.

Losing your pet means the cutting of this bond, the tearing out of your life of all those sources of good feelings. The void left behind in you and your life hurts like an open wound, a wound you fear will never heal.

2. Talk About It.

Oh well has it been said,
that there is no grief
Like the grief that does not speak.

    Henry Wadsworth Longfellow

Please talk about all this! Talking with yourself will provide help in the grieving experience. When talking with yourself, describe exactly how you feel. Try to describe why you feel as you do. Expressing an experience verbally, out loud, helps to give it form, structures it so you can develop a sense of what you are dealing with. This removes some of the vagueness, the mystery, that can make a bad experience even worse. Talking with yourself is not a sign that you are beginning to slip mentally. It is a healthy device to sort things out, to understand what is happening to you.

Talk about your feelings with other people. You may

ask yourself, "But who will try to understand, or at least accept, your feelings?" The answer is that the people who you think care about you deserve at least a chance. Your family, your friends, give them a chance if you can. If their responses are not helpful, ask yourself if you know anybody (maybe not even very well) who loves pets as you do. As you know, all people who have pets do not necessarily love them. However, a person who truly loves pets would probably be open to you, even if he or she has never lost one. People who love pets can imagine what it must be like to lose one.

If you have a relationship with God, talk to God. After all, prayer is just another word for talking to God. When you're by yourself or at a religious service, let God know how you're doing and what you're feeling. Describe the moments that are the most painful and the memories that continue to haunt you. Talk as you would to a best friend.

In your conversations do not be afraid to talk about the good times. How Prince used to pester you to throw that frisbee for him to fetch. He would follow you all over the yard, hold it in is mouth, nudging you with it. How Velvet would crouch on the seat of the kitchen chair, watching you as you prepared a meal. And how pleasant it was to know that she was enjoying her meal as you were enjoying your own. Maybe it hurts to remember those moments. But they were all a part of the life you shared together, and they all really matter. Remember, nothing about you and your pet is too large or too small to talk about — either with yourself, with God, or with other people.

III. The Experience
of Grieving

1. The Delayed Reaction.

People often have experiences after the loss of a pet which perhaps they didn't expect. The first reaction to loss is frequently a feeling of shock, of numbness. Sometimes, for a little while, a person can even refuse to believe that their pet is really dead. There is nothing unusual about any of this.

Many people are surprised when they find themselves feeling not much of anything after the loss of their pet. A lack of feeling at this point is really a lack of grieving. This absence of emotion sometimes can persist for weeks and even months. From this a person may come to the conclusion that, ''I guess I'm stronger than I thought.'' Or, one might wonder, ''What's wrong with me? Don't I have any real feelings?'' Should you find yourself in such a predicament, please don't feel ashamed. Such attitudes as these are entirely normal and you *can* expect to experience delayed reactions to your loss. At some unexpected time, your pent up feelings are very likely to suddenly rush out and overwhelm you. We can usually be on the alert for such delayed reactions if we understand that they are most likely to happen in a context or setting in which strong emotional associations are present.

2. The Impact of Special Occasions.

Those "special days" can be particularly difficult to get through without experiencing some bad moments. Christmas, Hanukkah, your birthday, your pet's birthday, the anniversary of your pet's death: these can recall all sorts of strong emotional associations.

At your annual birthday dinner Angel was always there to sample a bit of the first piece of cake you cut, her little pink tongue licking delicately at the sugary frosting. Then she would look up at you with those bright cat eyes and suddenly leap into your lap! Angel was run over a week after your last birthday. You don't feel much like having a birthday dinner this year.

It is Christmas Eve. It's time to hang up the Christmas stockings. You open the box where they are kept. There is Buddy's stocking that you hung with the others every Christmas Eve. Suddenly you are holding the stocking and crying. All this time you though you had "gotten over" Buddy's death, which had occurred nearly a year ago.

People experiencing these reactions in "emotionally loaded" situations require loving patience from themselves and from others. They are not behaving foolishly or irrationally. This behavior is a natural part of the grieving process.

3. Answering A Young Person's Questions.

What do you say when your little son asks you, "But where is Jerry now?" He knows that you buried your German shepherd under the big lilac bush in your yard. Often young people are not given the opportunity to share in the process of grieving. Even though they may be only on the periphery of the experience, the young person is likely to be feeling some fear and confusion over something they may not fully understand. Perhaps they too need to be comforted. Maybe they may even need to be permitted to *give* comfort.

If there is a young person present in the situation of pet loss, anticipate that they may want to be a part of it. Listen gently and carefully to their questions. Answer them truthfully, being careful not to go beyond what the young person really wants to know.

If you have children or younger brothers or sisters, you

can expect questions about the loss of a pet. What you truly believe will be the perfect answer.

4. What To Do About Guilt And Anger.

Are you feeling guilty about something associated with the loss? Maybe painful thoughts and questions keep recurring in your mind. "Should I have allowed the vet to put Tommie to sleep? Maybe we should have tried one more operation?" "Why did I have to take Sparky out for a walk that late? If I had taken her out at the usual time she would never have been hit by that truck. The driver couldn't even see her! It was really my fault!" Please don't blame yourself. We are only human, after all, unable to foresee the future and without the power to always structure events as we would like them to be. You have every right to protest the loss, but you are not guilty of causing it.

Or you may be remembering all those times when you were less than patient. You wish you could take back every slap you gave Rusty when he would chew on your magazines. Or that time you shoved Silky out of your bedroom and kept her out for a week when she jumped up on you and tore a jagged rip in your new cashmere slacks. She was only glad to see you! Now you know you didn't get any vindictive satisfaction out of those episodes. You were only doing what seemed appropriate at the moment. And those events represent at most a very tiny fraction of your times together!

Regrets are normal and often painful, but don't let them warp and darken your perspective of the past. The good times were so much more important than the not-so-good times!

Perhaps you find yourself getting angry about the loss of your pet. Your dear companion was taken away from you. Nobody checked with you first or asked your permission. And now you're left behind holding the pain! How grossly unfair!

As a matter of fact, this *is* pretty unjust. It is natural to be angry in a situation like this. Do not be afraid to express your anger right out loud.

However, try not to make other people the target for the anger you rightly feel. Even if the veterinarian wasn't as careful or tactful as he might have been, shouting at him will not make you or him feel any better. Maybe your husband doesn't really understand cats the way you do. Yet he didn't want Tiger to die, even if he did complain about spending all that money on canned cat food. Perhaps your friend did forget to close the gate, and Smokey wandered out of the yard and never came back. Your friend feels bad enough as it is. Think how much worse she will feel if you get angry with her. Making her feel worse should not make you feel any better.

Don't smother your anger though. And try not to feel guilty for feeling angry! Talk about it. Sometimes it helps to do some physical exercise to release some of the tension. Take a walk, explore a shopping mall, play some tennis, do a little gardening. And remember, you have every right to be angry.

5. Handling The Painful Sadness.

There's that sadness that hangs over you like a painful cloud all day and even at night. Sometimes you experience it even in your dreams. This kind of depression is to be expected after a serious loss. However, knowing this doesn't make it any easier to bear. The sadness goes with you wherever you are. And it has an endless quality that is downright frightening! Will this terrible feeling ever stop, or even lessen a little? You have an awful suspicion that it won't.

The day drags on. How lonely it is in the house all day without Flossie to keep you company. Her very presence helped you through the housework. Now you can hardly get through it, especially the bedroom where her empty basket stares at you.

Since your wife died two years ago, Blackie had been your only real friend. It's so hard to come back from work to an empty house. When you open the door you can almost hear his welcoming bark. Now there is nothing but silence. You are tempted to turn right around and run away.

Maybe school *was* rough, but you could always count on that walk afterwards with Lucky. Lucky never criticized and always understood. That is, until he died in his sleep three weeks ago. Now, nobody understands.

You wake up at night and realize that your feet are cold. They never were when Chrissie was there to keep them warm. Suddenly you remember how you felt when you held her as she choked for breath before she died. Now you are cold all over. How are you supposed to go on living with this feeling of painful emptiness? It seems to be everywhere.

Perhaps you are telling yourself, "I ought to be able to fill this emptiness. After all, I have family and friends, I have work." People tell you that you can at least *distract* yourself from your grief. Again, the idea that there must be something wrong with *you* that you are feeling so bad about losing your pet.

Aren't other things, or people, supposed to be more important? The answer is, "No, they're not necessarily more important; they're different." We don't miss something on account of what it was. We miss something because of what it meant in our lives.

Your pet was a very important part of your life. The people you know, and especially *you,* must respect this. The fact that you cared so much is a great compliment to you. You were brave and sensitive enough to invest your emotions unselfishly, not simply to take what you could get from an essentially defenseless being. People who say such love is basically selfish are greatly mistaken. Your relationship with your pet was of the healthiest kind, and many people would do well to imitate it. You didn't take from your pet. Your pet freely gave what he or she possessed in order to make your life a better and happier one. And, as in any good relationship, you did the same for your pet.

Of course, you didn't always give the same things to

each other. But, altough Tippy couldn't speak English, he spoke to you all the same. The special look in his eyes, those various barks, all the different types of body language, these things told you more than any verbal conversations could have done.

Well, what about this painful sadness? First of all, know that you are not alone. Pet lovers everywhere understand what you are going through. I understand what you are feeling. We all feel with you. Realize that, although we may not be physically near you, emotionally and in spirit we are right by your side. This book is a symbol of our keeping you company in your grief. Through it, I, all of us, are gently suggesting things that you can do to help yourself through your time of bereavement. And we are quietly mentioning ways in which others can assist you in this most difficult period.

Finally, we are hoping and waiting for that time in the future when your pain will have eased somewhat, when its sharpness is softer and less difficult to bear. For that time will come when you look back at this anguish and wonder how you ever got through it. Yet the time will never come when you forget about your pet, nor would we want it to. No one who loves a pet ever gets entirely "over" the loss.

There will be situations where you will get a sudden temporary return of the distress. But those occasions will get fewer and fewer, and farther and farther apart. The agonizing sadness turns gradually into a quiet sorrow which, in turn, will slowly recede, like a wave withdrawing back into the body of the ocean. Memories which caused you to feel immense heartache will eventually bring an awareness of peace.

Other things become meaningful again, and you will be less preoccupied with your loss. You even begin to feel moments of happiness — something you considered impossible a while ago. You are healing.

IV. The Companion.

> *How many . . . creatures on earth*
> *Have learned the simple dues of*
> *fellowship . . .*
>
> *Elizabeth Barrett Browning*

The Companion.

Now, what if your pet had an animal companion? This will add a different dimension to your grief experience, for the pet left behind will grieve for his or her lost companion.

Jimmie and Jinnie were raised together from the time when they were kittens. The three of you became inseparable friends. What good times you had, playing eternally with that old ball you gave them on their first Christmas. And how completely you could relax together, you on the couch, the two of them, limp and drowsy, snuggled next to you and to each other. Last week Jinnie died after a brief illness, despite everything you and the vet could do. Now Jimmie restlessly wanders all over the house, looking for Jinnie. The two of them always ate from their private dishes side by side. Jimmie has lost his appetite, barely touching even the most tempting foods. Sometimes he simply looks up into your face, all but saying, "Where *is* Jinnie? She *has* to be somewhere."

Well, now you have someone who is sharing your painful experience in his own way. Talk to your pet and give him or her any comfort you can. You will be comforting each other. Be sure not to allow the pet to be alone much. Even by leaving the radio playing while you are away, your pet will be less lonely in your absence.

You had two border collies, bundles of energy and affection. Sometimes they scrapped, sometimes they played. They were a lot of fun to be around. Yesterday Dan was chasing a squirrel and ran out of the yard and right in front of a car. He was killed instantly. Seeing this happen was like a nightmare from which you can't awaken, no matter how hard you try. Since last evening, Dolly has been hiding in a corner, whining a little every once in a while, trembling all over. She saw it happen too, heard the shriek of brakes and that other, terrible sound of impact. You come out of a daze enough to talk gently to her, coax her to let you hold her. Finally you and she are linked in a new way, like travelers who have survived a disaster together.

Sometimes a bereaved pet can exhibit unusual behavior. Such a pet might seem to be avoiding your presence or even run away from you. Or a previously affectionate pet may appear indifferent to you or even hostile. Remember that a bereaved pet is probably experiencing immense bewilderment. Something big is suddenly missing from his or her life, just as it is missing from yours. But the pet can't possibly understand what has actually happened, even though he or she may have witnessed the event. Such a pet can feel confused, disoriented, panic stricken, even aggressive.

Try to be patient with him or her, just as you are trying to be easy with yourself. You can help each other, even if it means simply keeping each other company. You are experiencing the pain of loss together, each in your own way, and that is terribly difficult for each of you. You do, however, have a friend who truly understands. And your pet has you.

IV. Healing.

> *The grave itself is but a*
> *covered bridge*
> *Leading from light to light,*
> *through a brief darkness.*
>
> *Henry Wadsworth Longfellow*

Healing.

As I said earlier, you will notice that the pain of your grief will gradually lessen as time goes by. Sharp pangs will still strike you from time to time, but the overall experience gets softer, and slowly recedes from your consciousness. Of course, you will never forget the last one. But now perhaps you are ready to deal with some issues which must have your attention eventually.

For example, what are you going to do with your pet's effects? Pebbles had her own special basket and blanket, and her food dishes and toys. Rusty's brushes, collar and lead, and favorite ball are all in your bedroom dresser drawer. You need to decide whether you want to dispose of them permanently or keep them. Perhaps they are items you really don't want around. Or, maybe you would like to keep them permanently in memory of your pet. Any decision that you thoughtfully come to in this matter will leave you feeling peaceful.

If your pet is buried in your yard or in a pet cemetery (see appendix), don't be embarrassed to visit the grave. Some people continue to visit the graves of their pets for years, particularly on special occasions. And there is nothing strange about talking to your pet when making these visits, either silently and right out loud. Some people don't want to visit their pet's graves, but many do. You should follow your feelings in this area.

Well, what about acquiring a new pet? I do not, of course, recommend the "instant replacement" routine. Well meaning friends or relatives often have the overwhelming urge for you to acquire a brand new pet to quickly "fill" the empty place left behind by the lost one. Although understandable, this is a mistake. In the shock of your first grief, you are not ready for a new pet relationship. In fact, at that point, having a new pet can even complicate your grief, possibly causing resentment and other types of stress. However, the time will probably come when all by yourself you begin to feel like having a pet again.

Please don't feel disloyal if you want another pet. You are not trying to replace your lost one at all. You are simply ready for a new pet relationship, which means it is time for you to have one. Your lost pet is ''gone but not forgotten;'' yet that doesn't mean that you must shut yourself off from the happiness of a new relationship. Every relationship has its uncertainties, but the love it generates is worth all the risks.

Perhaps, however, you really don't want another pet — ever. That's all right, too. Only you should decide where and when to invest your emotions. You are by far the best judge when it comes to yourself. So, follow your feelings. Don't force yourself into a new relationship, no matter what anyone says.

Finally, whatever decisions you come to, remember that you are not powerless in the situation of grieving. There *are* areas of your life where you can exert control. Remember, too, that all of us who love pets are ''pulling for you.'' We know what you have been going through, and we understand your feelings even now. We won't desert you and don't you desert us. The world of pet lovers has its share of disaster and tragedies, but it has a dimension of happiness to life unknown to those outside that world.

Appendix

Appendix

The choice of a place of "final rest" for a pet will differ according to personal taste and resources available. Some pets have burial places in a family's backyard, others on a friend's farm. If these options are unavailable or unacceptable, finding a final resting place for your pet can pose a real problem.

One option would be a discussion with your veterinarian. Such a person may be able to provide you with a number of suitable choices.

You might wish to consider the additional option of a "pet cemetery." A pet cemetery is simply a piece of land set aside specifically for the interment of pets. Most pet cemeteries are relatively small and privately owned and maintained. They are similar in many ways to cemeteries for people. Many offer private burial plots, a variety of repositories (including caskets), and several types of markers (such as plaques or gravestones). Some feature burial certificates, viewings, embalming, and cremation. Most allow unlimited personal visits to the grave site after the burial.

As is the case in any business, the quality of services and merchandise may vary from one pet cemetery to another. From my personal experience I can say, however, that many are owned and operated by sympathetic people who love animals.